"I Know What You're Really Thinking"

Reading Body Language Like a Trial Lawyer

By

Marc Mogil, J.D.

ISBN: 1-4107-0260-X (E-book)
ISBN: 1-4107-0261-8 (Paperback)
ISBN: 1-4107-0701-6 (Dustjacket)

Library of Congress Control Number: 2002096438

This book is printed on acid free paper.

Printed in the United States of America
Bloomington, IN

1stBooks - rev. 01/31/03

Author's Acknowledgements

I wish to thank those in my past for unwittingly assisting in this project with both their verbal and non-verbal communications; my Mom for a lifetime of selfless caring and giving to her children and grandchildren; my brother Roy Mogilanski, whose editorial talents, support and ongoing love profoundly aided in this and other endeavors; my dear friend and a noted Psychoanalyst, Barbara Kaplan, who unselfishly volunteered her immeasurable clinical insights, research, time, suggestions, and reading drafts; and my wife, Terry, son Matt, and my "always happening" teenaged triplets, Eric, Josh and Rachel, for making my very lively life worth living.

<u>Dedication:</u>

This book is dedicated to my loving family, without whom nothing worthwhile attained in this life would have been possible.

CAVEAT FOR THIS BOOK

"You can fool all of the People some of the time
You can fool some of the People all of the time
But you can't fool all of the People all of the time."

—Abraham Lincoln, 1864

TABLE OF CONTENTS

PREFACE xi

I. AN OVERVIEW 1

II. MODES OF NON-VERBAL

COMMUNICATION 20

   1. GENERAL BODY POSITION 33

   2. CLOTHING AND GENERAL

      ACCESSORIES 38

   3. EYES 49

   4. SPECIFIC FACIAL GESTURES 62

   5. THE MOUTH AND FACIAL

   CAMOUFLAGING 65

   6. LIPS 76

   7. HAND POSITION OR MOTION 78

   8. SPEED OF RESPONSE............................ 81

   9. CHIN AND JAW POSITION.......................85

10. THE ARMS..86

11. THE LEGS..88

12. HEAD MOTIONS 89

III. Non-Verbal Signals: Territoriality and Zones of

Privacy 93

IV. The Ideal Candidates for Practicing Non-Verbal

Communication 100

V. Test Yourself! 105

VI. Conclusion 111

REFERENCES 121

INDEX 125

PREFACE

This book was originally intended purely as an aide to the trial practitioner, based upon my prior years of practicing jury trial law as a Special Prosecutor, defense lawyer, New York State judge, and jury selection consultant. Much of that time was spent interviewing people in varying situations (as witnesses, suspects and clients), and observing as a trial judge numerous lawyers undertaking the process of *"voir dire"* in criminal trials.[1]

These activities yielded a plethora of information to me as a long-time aficionado of "kinesics"[2] and

---

[1] *Voir Dire* is the process by which attorneys have the opportunity to question and observe prospective trial jurors before final selections are made.

[2] Formally defined as "the study of nonlinguistic bodily movements, such as gestures and facial expressions, as a systematic mode of communication, *The American Heritage® Dictionary of the English Dictionary, 4th ed.,* New York: Houghton Mifflin Company, 2000.

"proxemics"[3] — the former being the science of body language and reading human postures, facial expressions, and other motions that convey unconscious messages; the latter, (developed and first used by noted researcher E.T. Hall), meaning a system of reading the space people unconsciously place around themselves, setting up "zones of privacy," spatial relationships, and territoriality as part of the study of body language and non-verbal communication.

However, after reviewing my notes from interviews, client files, judicial trial books, juror questionnaire summaries, files as a jury consultant, and various writings on the subject, it became clear that not only could body language assist young attorneys or law

---

[3] Formally defined as "the study of the cultural, behavioral, and sociological aspects of spatial distances between individuals, *The American Heritage® Dictionary of the English Language, 4th ed..* New York: Houghton Mifflin Company, 2000."

students, it could also be of great aid in almost every other non-legal endeavor. I therefore have expanded my intended scope to add situations and observations that would assist in everyday life.

The science that began in earnest in 1969-1970 (after Charles Darwin's groundbreaking first study of human gestures in 1872[4]), came in the United States with the publication of Julius Fast's *Body Language*[5], Luscher's *Color Test*[6], *and* Birdwhistell's *Kinesics and Context*[7], and has become a specialty in the last 30 years that is greatly expanding. Relating specifically to jury selection, former City College of New York Professor Jay Schulman was among the first to lead a team of social scientists in the early 1970's, aiding the lawyers for "radical defendant" trials (i.e. – "The

---

[4] For an available in-print edition, see Darwin, Charles, *The Expression of Emotions in Man and Animals,* New York: St. Martin's Press, 1980.

[5] Fast, Julius, *Body Language,* New York: Evans & Co., 1970.

[6] Luscher, Max, *Color Test,* New York: Pocket Books, Inc., 1971.

Chicago Seven," "Father Berrigan," "Angela Davis," etc.), leading to a detailed systematic loose-leaf jury selection manual for equally radical attorneys. This work-in-progress eventually saw publication.[8] These observations are now of great use to the general public, and could be most helpful applied to all occupations and personal situations, not just the law.

It is for this reason that I have modified my original outline, and geared this work also towards those who have not had the opportunity of trying to "read" people merely by interviewing or observing them as trial lawyers. By following the concepts to be discussed, the reader will be able to begin to read body language just like a trial lawyer.

---

[7] Birdwhistell, Ray L., *Kinesics and Context*, Philadelphia: University of Pennsylvania Press, 1970.

[8] Krauss, Elisa and Bonaro, Beth (eds.) *Jurywork: Systematic Techniques Volumes 1 and 2*, 2nded., New York: National Jury Project, 1992.

I wish to make clear, however, that this book is not designed to practice law in any way, but rather primarily to coax the reader to think like a skilled trial lawyer. Neither intended to be an exhaustive compendium of the scientific studies that have confirmed those observations I have made, nor an illustrated dictionary or encyclopedia of body language gestures, since that has already been done: those studies abound elsewhere and are generally not geared for a layperson.[9] I therefore take full responsibility for my *own* conclusions from my varied careers, unless otherwise stated.

---

[9] For an excellent and up-to-date compendium of scientific sources, I refer you to Givens, Robert B., (Ph.D.) *The Nonverbal Dictionary of Gestures, Signs & Body Language Cues (From Adam's-Apple-Jump to Zygomatic Smile),* Spokane, Washington: Center for Nonverbal Studies Press, ©2002, and Morris, Desmond, *Body Talk,* New York: Crown Trade Paperbacks, 1994.

Chapter I

An Overview

"The unconscious of one human being can react upon that of another without passing through the conscious."
— *Sigmund Freud*

Picture this purely fictional scenario: you are outside Interrogation Room Blue-206 at the Central Intelligence Agency (CIA) Headquarters in Langley, Virginia, which is a small "office," with many hidden micro-cameras and very well-concealed devices for surreptitious viewing, body temperature measurement, motion monitors and listening devices of all types. A person suspected of selling documents to a foreign government sits comfortably alone about to be interviewed as a potential spy. He is unrestrained, but there is only a chair for him to sit on...no desk or obvious one-way mirrors or recording machines viewable.

Prior to the interviewer entering the locked room, 17-20 CIA physicians, physiologists, psychiatrists, body language experts, and computer operators take their respective positions at various separate computer terminals and other hyper-modern monitoring machinery outside the room, and elsewhere in the building. These can, and will, continually and unknown to him measure the suspect's pulse rate, respiration rate, blood pressure, blink counts, body temperature changes, galvanic skin responses, vocal tone signature changes, and micro-movements and gestures. The computers do it all from afar. There is no typical polygraph machine in the room, since they do not wish the suspect to take any possible defensive physiological measures should he have been trained to endure more "normal" lie-detector tests in order to produce "false negative" results.

He also will be videotaped on all of these cameras from seven or eight different angles, including head-on close-up, from left and right at 45 degrees (full body), from the top directly over his chair, and full body from about 10 feet away. These tapes are capable of being replayed later at speeds of down to *one-tenth* the original, picking up the slightest motions of any part of the torso, head, any part of the face, or extremities. These motions will then be measured by the computers using an invisible "grid" system, which runs thermally-based lines horizontally and vertically throughout the entire room, visible to the cameras and computers, but not the suspect.

Marc Mogil, J.D.

Before the interrogator enters, all systems are switched on, and the many computers started for 5 minutes of monitoring, in order to obtain a "baseline" of non-pressure readings on the subject. These then continue throughout the interview, and for 5 minutes *after* the session ends, with the suspect still in the room.

After a very thorough interrogation, in which the suspect apparently gave answers that would have thoroughly convinced a non-experienced observer that he was totally innocent of the accusations against him, the "company's" Deception Detection Body Language Computer Program (DDBLP 1.1.2) provides print-outs clearly showing our suspect is lying at every crucial stage of the interview. The observers have already concluded that, purely from their visual analysis of his

body language alone.[10]

Does all of this make sense? Probably not now, but

I guarantee that you will understand all of it by the

end of this book!

Whether consciously understood or not, we use —

to various extents — non-verbal communications to

interpret the feelings, intent and meaning of strangers

and friends, of co-workers, bosses, politicians on

television, and even people passing in the street.[11]

The following second example shows how even

those among us who feel we have absolutely no such

observational talents are usually mistaken in this

---

[10] I highly recommend, Vrij, Aldert, *Detecting Lies and Deceit: The Psychology of Lying and the Implications for Professional Practice,* Chichester (UK): John Wiley & Sons, Ltd. (Europe), 2000; and regarding behavioral clues and a "Lie Catching Checklist," Ekman, Paul, *Telling Lies – Clues to Deceit in the Marketplace, Politics and Marriage,* W.W.Norton & Co., 2001, at pp. Appendix-353, 357.

[11] See, for example, two excellent studies on the subject by Morris, Desmond, *Bodytalk: The Meaning of Human Gestures,* New York: Crown

belief: it is merely a question of degree. For instance, consider this scenario:

Two people, a man and woman in their 20's, sit directly opposite from each other at a corner of a dimly lit Starbucks™ coffee shop. Their table is small and round and in a corner location, and the coffee cups (porcelain, and not throwaway containers) between them are untouched and moved to an edge of the table. Reviewing them physically from top to bottom, their heads are with 12 inches of each other, absolutely flush and level with each other's, their eyes are widely open; their shoulders are perfectly square to each other, the woman has her hand on the man's forearm which rests on the table, their knees are so close that they almost touch, their discourse is filled with whispered conversation and smiles back and

Trade Paperbacks, 1995; Morris, Desmond, *Gestures: Their Origins and* forth, and they appear oblivious to the activities of people at neighboring tables.

What can we conclude by their body language, even though not privy to so much as a *word* of their conversation? [12]

Most of us would agree that it can be safely assumed that is not a business meeting, that by asking for regular cups and saucers they expect to remain for more than just a brief time, that these people are emotionally involved and attracted to one another, that there exists a warmth and openness between them, and that despite the high quality of the

---

Distribution, New York: Stein and Day, 1980.

[12] [A word of caution regarding attempts at analyzing non-verbal communications: aside from the studies done in the field, it has been my experience that each nation or culture manifests different signals and gestures, sometimes meaning things *diametrically* opposed to those we in America are accustomed to. This is also true regionally, even within our own country, from north to south, from rural to urban. Thus, a caveat to those seeking to apply the examples and principles set forth within this book — know who you are attempting to "read," and what their "baseline" or usual non-verbal actions entail before attempting to extrapolate meaning from a particular non-verbal communication.]

Starbucks™ coffee, it is secondary to their spending romantic time with each other.

Thus, by merely observing their actions over less than five minutes, many valuable conclusions can be made, which are transferable in life to everyday situations involving employment, meeting and judging people, ascertaining whether peoples' words match their true feelings, and general non-verbal communication. You see, you already can function within the general parameters of the concepts of body language. It takes no magic: merely a new way of regarding your surroundings.

A caution once again before proceeding further: there are immense cultural differences in which both body language and kinesics vary. For instance: people from Mediterranean cultures and Eastern European Jews tend to be very facially expressive and utilize their hands, arms and gestures far more in discussion, while those from Asia or Northern or Western Europe tend to use far less body motion or emotion while speaking. Keep in mind their "baseline" of non-stressful usual conversation in a given context must be carefully evaluated before any attempt at body language can occur.

Another example, and we'll begin to see how the average person intuitively knows *much* more about "kinesics" (the art of reading body language) than previously believed:

Presume you are an invisible observer at a business meeting, watching two executives (Smith and Jones) enter a meeting room to work out a technical problem within the company. You have neither any idea of their respective status on their corporate ladder, nor their titles. They are about the same age and of the apparent same cultural background, both wearing conservative business attire. As they enter the conference room together and close the door, Smith takes a seat at the head of a very long rectangular table in the largest and highest chair in the room, while Jones says nothing and sits next to him at the nearest side position. After a short, calm and apparently polite verbal interchange, Smith stands up and takes off his suit jacket, slings it on a neighboring empty chair, and thereafter sits in shirt sleeves, placing his body high and forward in his already higher chair and leaning clearly towards his colleague, with his arms parallel resting on the table and pointing directly towards Jones, fixing his eyes squarely at him throughout; Smith seems to be gazing directly at Jones' eyes during the interchange almost without ceasing contact, and repeatedly points a finger at his colleague for emphasis. Jones frequently interrupts the stare and looks away.

On the other side, Jones keeps his jacket on in the warm room when Smith takes his off. Jones leans backwards and seems to slightly slump in his chair and rolls it a bit away from the table. Jones, in between taking brief notes, (which Smith does not), does indeed verbally speak his mind, yet folds his hands on the table and lowers his eyes at times during the conversation, especially when Smith speaks and stares. Additionally, when Jones speaks, Smith covers his own lips with his hand. Jones also plays with a ring he is wearing while speaking, looking at times at the ring rather than at Smith.

What we can conclude from this exchange, in very general terms, is the following:

1. Smith is the higher in title (and dominant) of the two executives in the corporation;

2. Smith's taking his jacket off (even if he wasn't warm) signified he felt he had the power to treat Jones informally, while Jones did not feel the same way about Smith;

3. Smith's sitting in a higher chair and attempting to place his body even higher, put his eye level *above* that of Jones, creating an unconscious feeling of dominance;

4. Smith's leaning towards Jones the entire time was a body cue that he was taking control of the conversation, and had no intention of backing off, while Jones moving his chair slightly away from the table and sitting flush and low in it seems a defensive or submissive posture;

5. Smith's keeping his arms pointed at Jones and pointing his finger for emphasis were gestures of assertiveness and "control," as pleasant as the conversation might have otherwise been (the proverbial "point" of the ancient spear);

6. Smith's incessant stare (to be dealt with later in greater detail) is a clear sign of dominance, assertiveness and control in human interaction, and challenged Jones to either say something cogent to change his mind, or back off;

Jones' glancing downward was a sign of subliminal submittal and resignation to whatever Smith was proposing as a conclusion to their discussion;

Smith's covering his lips with his hand when Jones spoke unconsciously meant he did not wish to hear any more from Jones at that point.

Marc Mogil, J.D.

Your own conclusions? I assume you guessed most of these items in the above example yourself! A good cognitive start, since non-verbal communication is based mainly upon common sense and the now non-indisputable conclusion that these symbols or cues to be discussed are in most instances *uncontrollable* physiological micro-rapid reactions of the body's nervous system and muscles reacting to certain external stimuli. Since most human gestures and communications are unconscious (unless practiced as a form of deliberate or professionally taught interrogation techniques or deception), learning the basics of the human reactive mind in any interaction with others is central to an understanding of the tools that we can use.

A perfect example of the use of non-verbal body language, position, and level of eye contact to dominate a situation, occurred with the late former President Lyndon B. Johnson. It was commonly known that when he assumed the Presidency, he modified "Air Force One" so that his private office cabin contained a large, semi-circular desk surrounding a chair that many called his "throne," since it was so large and tall.

However, the really important part of the system was a hidden button that the President could use to hydraulically *lift* it to different levels, used mainly so that his eye level would always be at or above those to whom he was speaking in that cabin. Obviously, President Johnson was well aware of the importance of eye contact and relative elevation in body language during decision-making and influencing people.[13]

Let's try another example:

Marc Mogil, J.D.

Imagine that you are at a professional baseball game on a hot summer's day (baseball players, managers and umpires being a wondrous source of body language). It is the bottom of the 9th inning, the score is tied, two out, with a runner at third base. The batter has hit a ground ball to the third baseman, who — after juggling it for a moment — makes a desperate and late throw to home plate in an attempt to prevent the runner coming in from third base from scoring and winning the game.

In your expert opinion (from 100 yards away), the runner was clearly safe, having beaten the late throw. However, after delaying a moment, the home plate umpire (less than 5 feet from the play) makes a fist with his thumb protruding (signifying, in simple baseball body language, an "out.")

---

[13]   USAF   Museum,   Presidential   Aircraft   Collection,

Immediately, the manager of the "victimized" player runs out of the dugout, waving his arms wildly, putting his body squarely within inches of the umpire, shouting, his face turning red, throwing his cap to the ground, while kicking up dirt on the umpire's shoes. The manager is then escorted from the field arm-in-arm by two of his coaches after the umpire gestures another "out" sign and points to the dugout.

Conclusion? An easy one, isn't it? It is clear that the manager is expressing his great pleasure and admiration to the umpire for the hard work he has done in the game, and is inviting him to his home for a Sunday barbeque, while the umpire in turn is warmly accepting and points to the dugout to suggest the manager rest out of the heat of the summer sun. *Do*

---

you really believe that was what the body language said, without even hearing a word?

Of *course* that wasn't what was said! The manager was most likely telling the umpire, in clearly raw, succinct and caustic language, that the believed a visit to the ophthalmologist was in order for the umpire, since the runner was clearly safe. Waving his arms, tossing the cap on the ground and kicking dirt on the umpire were the final signs of anger and disrespect for the decision. When the umpire responded by signaling "out" a second time and pointing to the dugout, he was clearly throwing the manager out of the game. Even a non-baseball fan could have interpreted that one, but the signs utilized begin to form a clear non-verbal language. This example is so clear, that we don't even consciously realize that no words came to our ears to help us convey meaning.

What is important to remember always in any study of body language, in my opinion, is that the human organism physiologically signals a truthful response each and every time, *however brief*, before the person makes or is able to make the conscious choice of whether to tell the truth, react, or to deceive. Once the observer understands this, learning the various symbols of the body's cues and how to watch for them — one is well on his way towards learning to "read people." Jury Consultants, for example, use "focus groups" to test these skills in specific cases. It is almost like learning a new language, since we look for signs in people that were never before important to us. It is a matter of not just seeing, but *looking*.

Chapter II

Modes of Non-Verbal

Communication

Twenty-first century Americans, as do every other culture in the world, have a myriad of means by which they communicate, some more common and easily understood, and some requiring a degree of repetitive experience to fully comprehend.[14]

Be it by direct conversation, in writing, via videotape, audiotape, telephone, or silent motions of the body alone, humans unconsciously transmit their true feelings and desires. Those who learn to *observe* and interpret them, and not merely *see* them, are on

---

[14] Hinde, Robert A., *Non-Verbal Communication*, London: Cambridge University Press, 1972, (see especially p. 207).

the way to learning a new skill, and will have an advantage over those around them.

Obviously, written words on paper are impossible to analyze non-verbally (except analytically by a trained graphologist), since we cannot *see* the person express those written words in any concurrent manner; this is also true with an audio tape or telephone (except by Voice Stress Analysis, available and truly comprehensible now only to the intelligence community, like the FBI, CIA or in particular the National Security Agency (NSA) which specializes in intercepting and deciphering audible messages from all over the globe). However, direct conversations, videotaped statements, and singular body motions viewable by an observer send irrefutable signals that the person, unless very strenuously and consciously trained and almost brainwashed to control or

Marc Mogil, J.D.

manufacture them (i.e. – a CIA Field Agent or an especially skilled political candidate), subliminally and involuntarily transmits their true feelings, despite what their words may say to the contrary.

Think of common body signals we immediately recognize: a traffic police officer raising his open hand in the air, palm forward, signifying "stop;" a person flashing an "OK" sign — hand raised with the thumb and forefinger making the shape of a circle;[15] someone who is asked a question who responds by shaking his head from side-to-side, meaning "no," [but remember what I previously mentioned about cultural differences...in certain parts of the world, this signal means *just the opposite!]*; a person flashing a "V" for victory sign or a "thumbs-up" at a stranger, signifying

---

[15] Cultural differences are discussed elsewhere in this book; however, it is safe to say that if one tried this gesture in some countries overseas, it signifies the sign for a sexual orifice or an effeminate man!

a pleased and positive signal to another, [caution again — don't try this in the Far East unless you're looking for a black eye since it implies an pejorative sexual insult); a person at a conference table who suddenly pulls his chair away from the table, glances at the ceiling, and begins to smile, signifying someone who clearly disagrees vehemently and sardonically with whatever was just said by someone else at the table; someone on a witness stand who is asked after a string of difficult questions if he was implicated in a specific crime, who then momentarily covers his face with both hands, signifying a reluctance to verbally answer based upon some form of guilt, (this has indeed occurred in my presence, and is not solely within the purview of "Perry Mason" television reruns).

These are of course very simple and common signals that most of us have experienced and instantly recognize: but there exist many other much more subtle signs and signals or even verbal "covers" that can be gleamed from the posture, positioning or phraseology of a person, which can in fact *annihilate* the veracity of what they are saying, and give the experienced observer a true insight into what is *really* being said. This is a matter of what some have called "leakage," which is bodily signals that escape the control of the conscious mind.

For instance, any experienced judge or trial attorney becomes quite wary of certain specific opening words as answers from a witness on the stand or a potential juror, that serve to unconsciously give away the person's true feelings. I've learned throughout the years that in any question requiring a "yes" or "no" answer (such as, in a potentially controversial type of case, "Can you be fair towards this defendant owing to the violent nature of the crime alleged"), an answer that begins with, "I'll try..." or "I think I can..." or "I'll do my best..." mandates immediate further inquiry and gross skepticism, since it virtually *shouts* an unconscious pre-determination on the part of the person towards a formation of a negative conclusion. If not pursued, the outcome of the trial most certainly has already been decided during *voir dire.* This equivocal response is usually combined with one or more of the non-verbal symbols to be discussed in later chapters indicating the same sort of negativity towards the defendant.

Thus, verbiage and intonation itself, especially when combined with the benefit of accompanying body language, becomes important in interpreting what someone *really* has on his mind.

"People are more practiced in lying with words than with faces...This is probably because people are held accountable for their words..."[16]

Other non-verbal considerations are how a person is dressed and groomed, and what if anything they are carrying or wearing, or is attached to their clothing, that may signal non-verbal feelings that should be understood.

For instance, a person who appears late for a job interview with no excuse, in sloppy clothing, and with unkempt hair, yields an obvious conclusion: the person is either totally unaware or unmindful of both the proper attire and manners for a place of business.

---

[16] Ekman, Paul and Friesen, Wallace, *"Unmasking the Face,"* Englewood Cliffs, NJ: Prentice-Hall, Inc., 1975.

So, too, in a court case in which a government witness will be the only available witness regarding the believability of a contested accusation by a prosecutor, the wearing by a potential juror of an American flag lapel pin, organizational membership pin of certain types, a religious symbol, or — on the other hand — some sort of anti-authority pin or button, bespeaks their political, social or moral persuasion. Nothing a person carries or wears can be ignored, without the gravest of consequences.

I recall quite clearly that in my more than 25 years as a Special Prosecutor, Judge, defense lawyer and jury selection consultant, I looked (without exception) at any reading material the potential witness or juror carried into the room, since that too spoke reams about their education, state of mind, politics, and often potential receptiveness to a point of view, and a proclivity to carry a fair or unfair evaluation of what was about to happen into deliberations.

For instance, a person toting a highly technical or scientific journal for reading in free time, might be queried carefully about what level of proof they would require in a case, since a scientist or engineer might in fact have a far more strict or exacting level of proof than would be required under the law in the specific matter upon which they are being called to judge. Ofttimes, they are accustomed to the extraordinarily high proofs required in their careers.

So too, a person carrying a romance novel, a science fiction novel, a book about UFO's, or one on "the upcoming revolution in America," might be telling you that they are open to allowing their minds to be pliable and will consider all options, and not form opinions prior to considering all of the facts. I've found, too, that aficionados of flightful novels of fiction or spiritualism often are far more open to suggested factual scenarios that are at times unlikely in everyday life, as opposed to scientists, engineers, architects, statisticians, mathematicians, and those whose careers mandate an exactitude of analysis and a resultant matching of the facts.

I always took careful note of a person carrying or reading a Bible during free time, since someone of that devotional mindset most likely has pre-formed opinions of morality and credibility concerning different types of people which might sway unfettered deliberations. I ask myself: how would they react to the testimony of a cleric; how would they act with someone who never attends church or synagogue; how would they react to the concept of "an-eye-for-an-eye;" how would they feel about authority figures; how would they feel about someone from a diametrically different religion; would they attempt to take charge of the jury in deliberations utilizing a different standard than required by the law, etc? Do you see where this can go if taken to a logical conclusion?

A select few lawyers have been known to casually wander (or send someone) before formal appearance time into public areas where potential jurors may sometimes congregate, looking to see if someone is reading or carrying anything that might cause the need for later questioning, or saying something in a public area that should raise a red flag. Many attorneys, in fact, retain experts in jury evaluation and selection in major or high-profile cases, who sit incognito in the gallery and make observations that trial counsel cannot possible see, only having one set of eyes.

Of course, the entirety of a person — career, childhood and parents, current family, cultural background, religious upbringing, schooling, criminal record, relatives, experience with the justice system, etc., all bind together into a unique unconscious blend of signal transmittal, into whatever judgment a trained expert in non-verbal communication will make of it, since body language is context-oriented and context-sensitive.

Without delving into the almost immeasurable permutations and combinations of careers, experiences, and non-verbal signals, there exist far too many combinations of such symbols to discuss them all in any one book; thus, the ones I have chosen to deal with, even briefly, are those which have *repeatedly* and uniformly yielded a degree of success in the analysis of people who often say one thing, and mean another. Thinking about some of them will assist in building "antennae" for yourself that the average person does not have.

1. GENERAL BODY POSITION

The first symbol to consider is the person's general torso position relative to other parties with whom a conversation is being held. Discounting the first few moments credited to general "nerves" at what is often a stressful situation, the position of a person's shoulders ("angularity") is crucial. If, in response to a question, the shoulders remain square and directly facing the other party, this most usually signifies veracity and openness. Watch, if after a particularly difficult comment, the person's shoulders slightly move away at an angle from the other party. Should this occur, the response to that specific question must then be analyzed, since it indicates an evasiveness, anger or disdain, or a hesitancy to answer for some other reason.

Marc Mogil, J.D.

Known almost as a classic example of "angularity" was the late President Richard Nixon's habit of turning his shoulders up to between 45 and 90 degrees away from a person with whom he disagreed or disliked, even though he attempted to make pleasantries keeping his head and eyes looking directly at the person. This is evident from many news clippings taken of him during his Presidency.

The author (right) with the late President Richard Nixon. Note that the camera caught a rapid glance down and to the right by the President for an undetectable instant.

Another body position to view is the general lean or tilt of the torso: if it develops *towards* the other party, it implies an eagerness to cooperate, responsiveness, or an aura of truthfulness. A lean *away* or sitting back-tilt in a chair from the other party connotes just

35

the opposite, evasiveness, rejection, negative feelings and perhaps even hostility.

As we saw with the "Smith and Jones" example previously, as well as the President Johnson "throne chair" discussion, sitting high in one's seat, or attempting, as some have stated, to "contradict" gravity by body language by standing or sitting as straight up in their spot as possible, thus putting them and their eye contact higher than normal or others, implies an attempt to exert dominance over the situation, and often indicates either a certainty of one's feelings or a general demeanor of superiority or indignation. *Ergo*, a person on the witness chair or interview chair who suddenly sits up, square shouldered and tilting clearly towards the questioner, signifies someone who is telling the truth at that point, is somewhat aggressive and confident, and perhaps even angry about the nature of the question if such an affectation comes on suddenly. This is especially so in all instances if the body position was not as described *before* the question.

Another example is that of a person sitting directly opposite another at a luncheon table, which is occupied with sugar bowls, cream pourers, and salt and peppershakers. Moving any of these objects, or placing one's hands on the table far past the imaginary midline dividing the table between them, encroaching upon the other's unconscious "territory," is an assertive and aggressive movement, likely to be perceived as such, causing a disquieting discomfort to the "offended" party.

2. Clothing and General Accessories

There is an old axiom of "not judging a book by its cover." *Nonsense!* That may be true when evaluating the quality of a contemporary volume on library shelves, but it doesn't apply, for example, to a very rare antiquarian text, nor *certainly* to a person you are trying to read. How a person appears to others, how one dresses, and what items are accessorized or carried, tells a great deal about the person, consciously and unconsciously, since these involve choices made by the person regarding how to represent himself to the outside world. That's why, in situations where the sense of individuality is best repressed — such as the armed forces — uniforms are mandated, "making a commonality from many individuals," (translated on our American coins in Latin as *"E Pluribus Unum"*).

Clothing and colors worn is an important evaluator in reading the body language of a person.[18] Loud colors, "wild" ties, or conflicting colors or patterns, for example, connote an extrovert who wishes to be noticed. Softer pastels tend to reflect gentleness and more of an openness. Dark suits or jackets and tie versus open sport or "T" shirt connotes more of a conservative bent. Women's dresses or skirts versus casual slacks or jeans signify the same comparison. That seems clear. By a more subtle use of color as in an accessory, such as a man's tie, belt, shoes, socks or woman's scarf or hat, a distinct signal is sent.

As an example, I have always seen effective Prosecutors in a homicide trial wear ties with at least a little red in it at some important part of the proceeding (most often the summation), since I have concluded,

---

[18] See, again, Luscher's color studies as cited previously.

as others over the years, that red imparts an unconscious feeling of authority and believability upon the jury. So too with outer clothing colors of men or women attorneys: Prosecutors will tend to the darker, more formal and more serious, with gestures and voices to match; defense counsel will attempt more informal or lighter shades to unconsciously influence the jury that the formality the Prosecutor seeks is overdone: this will be accompanied by a more relaxed body posture, informal tones, and using his client's first name whenever possible.

On the other hand, someone wearing a conservative outfit with glaring red and green socks (if it isn't Christmas week), wants to be noticed and will tend to be the self-appointed spokesman for any group, since he does not wish to "fit in" to anyone's mold whatsoever.

So, too, with someone who is dressed all in black (except a Judge's robe, of course): such attire may impart a sense of extraordinary individualism, and perhaps a sense of superiority (or even imbalance) in a given situation. However, in this modern age, one must be careful regarding changing cultural mores: for example, in the current "dance club" scene in large cities (as I've learned from my college son in Michigan), it is common to see teenagers and those in their young 20's dress all in black at social functions, as it appears to have become something of a style. Therefore, *context* of the use of black, and the age of the wearer, becomes important in your analysis.

An older generation person wearing black is not trying to look "cool," as the teen at a New York City club, but may be telling you of a non-conformist streak.

As to *accessories*, look carefully at jewelry, the apparent *value* of the jewelry, lapel pins and materials, since each category sends immense messages about the person you are analyzing. An unusual amount of jewelry on a man or woman can imply either a sense of self-assuredness, or inferiority: it is at that point one must look for the concurrent body signals to tell you which it may be (leaving out mere "bad taste" for now), since it is an extreme in one direction or another.

Dealing with jewelry and the affect it can subliminally have on people observing, for example, brings to mind another example from my later years on the Bench: I knew a famous and quite able New York City criminal trial lawyer who, when he appeared before me in court, always carried TWO wristwatches with him on the first day of a trial and the selection of a jury, which he showed me before the jury pool entered the room: one was his usual solid gold Rolex® rimmed with diamonds, and one was an inexpensive rubber-strapped black Timex®. When he saw the socio-economic-status of the entering jury pool, he made a lightening evaluation and put on whichever watch would, in his own experience and opinion, show that "he was one of them" and cause him to better fit in and avoid disdain. He recognized that they would be sizing him up as much as he they.

Make no mistake: people in conversation or listening to someone in court or in a office setting always evaluate the person from head to toe, and whether they realize it or not, make conscious and unconscious judgments about what they see and what people wear. (Some also evaluate items of furniture in a person's office, even so minor as types of photo frames).

So, too, this particular attorney's clothing could either be a custom-tailored Armani™ suit, or far less expensive Sear's™ coordinates, depending on what opinion about himself he wished to impart to the jury, as I raised just previously.

In your own scan of people you are trying to "read," look for wedding bands, conservative ear rings on women, American flag lapel pins, religious insignia, Masonic pins, people carrying *The Wall Street Journal*, etc, that usually all signify their symbolic attitude in favor of the *status quo*, authority, loyalty and team playing. People whose body language and attire tend to the traditional and respectful to authority (i.e.- clothing that fits in to a particular situation without calling attention to themselves) are the people, in general, who will feel that "where there's smoke, there's fire."

Thus, jurors have often told me post trial, they felt that if there was enough for a Prosecutor to have brought charges or a police officer to have arrested someone, the defendant "must have done *something wrong* to get into that position" with such people, since authority figures would not have gone to the trouble of a trial if the defendant did not.

On the other hand, be on the lookout for ear rings of any type on men, radical tattoos on young people (not World War II vintage types which were common to servicemen in the 1940's), unusual hair styles, body "piercings," unusual or anti-establishment reading material, such as *"The Village Voice"* newspaper or *"The New Republic"* magazine, anti-government foreign-policy buttons, and rings on fingers upon which they are normally not worn. This can signify a streak of individuality, a "show me, Government!" mentality, or other trait that may indicate that the person will be anti-authority oriented and in general an outspoken and perhaps argumentative person.

A caution regarding tattoos: where in the more recent past it has signified an anti-establishment proclivity or a blue-collar badge of some sort, more and more very conservative or traditional young, affluent and educated people ("Yuppies") sometimes wish to have tattoos placed in visible spots, both men *and* women, and therefore their presence cannot yield by itself any definitive conclusions. Ironically, this is done in an effort to conform with the current social mores for their peer group. Putting them in context however, i.e.- present while wearing otherwise conservative clothing and business-like cropped hair, puts a more complete picture together like a jigsaw puzzle.

I've seen attorneys properly go on to ask about what people's favorite television shows were, as well as any daily reading material, hobbies, vacation preferences, and affiliations, all of which can lead an astute questioner to conclusions about a person's proclivities, opinions, abilities and willingness to form opinions away from a norm, and other traits not verbally said directly.

For example, one would expect different outlooks and standards from those who succinctly say (and appear proud) that they *never* watch network television or weekly sitcoms (some even state they don't own a television set) — only Public Broadcasting Educational Stations, if anything, to have very different mindsets upon almost everything. People who do difficult crossword puzzles as a regular hobby generally are far more exacting and analytical than those who say they collect rock star autographs. Those who are art museum sponsors are far more likely to be quite different than those who are members of a bowling league, in that the former in each above example tend to have a more traditionalist leaning, owing to their differences in socio-economic status. There are of course many other comparisons, but I think you begin to see what I have come across while attempting to complete a personality portrait of a person.

Not only are the verbal answers to these particular questions important, the body language which *accompanies* such innocent sounding words, of course, can say more than the language used itself.

3. EYES

The eyes, indeed as it has long been said, "are the windows to the soul." More specifically, it is the direction and movement changes of the eyes, as well as the surrounding orbital skin and facial and eye muscles and eyebrows, that make human eyes an almost infallible translator of inner feelings. This is most especially so in response to discussion or questioning, and a person accustomed to observing carefully has the uncanny ability to ascertain the true inner workings of another's mind.

It has been clear for many years now that there exists a direct correlation between emotion and eye and other body muscle movement, (as utilized in the polygraph or so-called "lie detector" machine which measures, among other things, galvanic (electric wave) skin response and changes in pulse, blood pressure, and rate of respiration).

These are conditioned upon the mind's physiological control of the muscles surrounding and controlling the eyes and other parts of the body, often within the first few tenths of a second. What we do, and do not do, relative to our current undertaking, is reflected particularly in the area of the eyes.[20]

The government certainly understands this. For instance, in those positions in which someone is responsible for another's safety, (for example, a Secret Service Agent guarding the President of the United States), one will almost always see them wearing very dark or mirrored sunglasses. Why? The darting and scanning nature of their required continuous and

---

[20] As cited in one of the leading books regarding the place of the eyes in body language — Nierenberg, Gerald I. & Colero, Henry H., *How to Read a Person Like a Book,* New York: Friedman, Michael Publishing Group, 2002.

unrelenting view of an area and of people is something they wish to conceal. If not, a potential assassin can detect it, since by seeing where Agents are looking, someone seeking to harm their charge would have a distinct advantage in timing when the Agents might be gazing elsewhere.

Human beings feel much more comfortable psychologically seeing the eyes of someone they are speaking with. That is generally why we feel most uncomfortable when someone wears dark lenses indoors or looks away at a crucial time.

This is not just a matter of "manners," but rather the mind's need to physically and continuously view another person's eyes, so that their motions and direction changes can be detected and unconsciously analyzed, along with listening to what others are really saying. As we progress here within the traits set forth within this book, our desire and rationale for viewing another's eyes will become hopefully more conscious than unconscious.

Conversely, to intentionally put someone in a position of unease, wearing anything that blocks or attempts to hide ones eyes is one way to attain that end.

As to judging what a person is thinking, and the veracity of their responses, an analysis of eye motion, lid response closure, and direction of view or gaze and its change when vocalization is made, is crucial to kinesics.[21] Observational skills once again.

For example, a person who is asked a question must consciously decide upon an answer, subsequent to his body unconsciously first signaling the truthful

---

[21] For an excellent study of the "direction of gaze" in body language, see Spiegel, Joseph P. & Machotka, Pavel, *Messages of the Body,* New York: The Free Press, 1974, at p. 274.

response. In a discussion, formal or informal, someone who looks away from a person while answering and who only occasionally glances back to the speaker (especially if the reactive gaze is *downward*), is signaling a degree of deception or discomfort. Instead, staring right back at the questioner, without squinting or other bodily movements, signals truthfulness or openness. In addition, squinting can signify anger in this circumstance, (think of Clint Eastwood's eyes in his movies when he becomes very angry).

However, *too much* direct staring can signify an attempt to convince someone of the veracity of what is being said (even though the person is overtly lying). A good liar knows what the examiner is looking for and, while it is impossible to suppress unconscious body language completely, one can attempt to create those signals that the truth is being told, when in fact it is not. Non-verbal signals of "betrayal of feeling" are commonplace, however.[22]

For example, if someone is interviewed and consciously wishes to be perceived as truthful, he will stare almost continuously at the questioner's eyes, keep his shoulders flush and parallel, lean forward in his chair, attempt never to divert his eyes at crucial times, keep his hands in front of him and exposed, and modulate his voice in such a way as to create a consistent and firm tone. But it is the *uninterrupted* staring that usually gives these people away.

Side glances, on the other hand, signify coyness, a consideration of evasiveness, or some interest by the viewer, while totally closing ones eyes even briefly after another's spoken words, signals that the response

---

[22] Mehrabian, Albert, *Nonverbal Communication*, Chicago: Aldine –

is, or will be, a difficult one for the person to give, and is a signal of a truly defensive gesture of the body. Whether it signifies embarrassment, dishonesty, or blocking out, correlates to the specific issues discussed.

In response to a query or statement, gazing *away,* especially in a *downward* direction, or rubbing one's eyes in response to a question, seems to signify outright dishonesty, since the body signals the muscles that it would rather not look directly at someone to whom they are about to lie. So too with eyes that suddenly appear to flit ("rabbit eyes"). Instead, raising one's eyes skyward and in response signals exasperation, real or feigned.

Another way to detect anxiety from the eyes is the rate of blinking: in the average person, 10-15 or so

Atherton, Inc., 1972, at p. 84.

blinks per minute seems to be the scientifically accepted average. A dramatic increase in that rate signals extraordinary nervousness, at the least. Thus, if a question elicits such a rapid rate response, one can properly assume that the responding person would rather not answer the question, be it from guilt, remorse or other emotion consistent with a less than full and direct openness.

The stare, as discussed earlier, is the most forceful way in body language to create emotional upheaval and an understanding that one's thoughts or motives are being scrutinized.

An excellent example of the effects of staring without interruption was done by a former early classmate of mine (whom I knew in the 1960's), after I had lost touch with him. Majoring in psychology, (now a respected Professor and Ph.D. at the University of

Rochester), his project was to learn what effects staring continuously at strangers in a public place would have.

If I recall the details correctly [it *was* some 30 or 35 years ago], this brave soul — neatly dressed in a conservative jacket and tie as not to be perceived as a potential physical threat, emotionally unbalanced person, or mugger — sallied forth for several weeks at various times and places into the depths of the New York City subway system, taking seats on un-crowded subway cars whenever possible. Understand that at the time, as now, the seats on New York City subways ran around the periphery of each car, each seat facing another seated person.

He chose to sit *directly opposite* total strangers, one-on-one, often in fairly empty train cars where people tend to give themselves a lot of space between their co-passengers and try desperately to avoid the eyes of strangers.

Some riders were reading books or newspapers, some reading the ads over the seats, some merely resting and awaiting their station stops, and some napping. As might be expected before major changes under former Mayor Rudy Guiliani, intruding on a stranger's space in public created a real risk of physical harm, (not an entirely unusual activity in a New York City subway train at that time).

Without exception, when each stranger finally caught the staring gaze of our budding psychologist, each one reacted in what I know now to be predictable ways. Some blocked their faces by raising up their reading materials to hide their eyes; some looked away nervously, and some eventually actually moved their seats or even changed cars to get away. Several individuals chose, (as could be predicted in a large experimental population coming from all sectors of society), to confront our experimental starer by shouting obscenities, qualities concerning the experimenter's alleged sexual preferences or family heritage and lineage, and fortunately only one or two actually stood and began to approach him, clearly annoyed enough to wish to bring things to blows. (As far as I know, my former classmate hasn't done any other experiments which might again have endangered his health.)

A final set of examples manifest how close observation of eye contact can say volumes about a group of people:

For instance, in any group in which one person is the more powerful or the leader, subordinates tend to make some sort of eye contact with that person after each important point as a sort of "check off" with the ultimate decision-maker.[23] This can be true both in a criminal interrogation of a group of people or gang members, where investigators are trying to sort out the hierarchy of the group, or in a corporate boardroom in which the decision-maker tactically decides *not* to disclose his identity by sitting on an out-of-the-way chair on the side of the room, instead at the head of the table, keeping relatively mum. If observed, his subordinates will *still* unconsciously make eye contact with him at pertinent parts of the discussion or negotiation, no matter how hard they try not to.

In sum, were I to select the one part of the body that gives most away in the art of reading body

---

[23] An excellent article on this very subject appeared reprinted in *The Topeka Capital-Journal*, by Franken, Stephanie (a Staff Writer for the *Pittsburgh Post-Gazette*), entitled *Body Language Often Tells Another Story*, April 30, 2001.

language, it would be the eyes. Our body's lack of total physical control of a very complex set of muscles and movement sensors for the eyes are central to successful kinesic analysis.

However, as previously stated, watch for an extreme in any of the symbols or gestures discussed throughout, as it can be a signal of an attempt to deceive.

"The eyes of man converse as much their tongues, with the advantage that the ocular dialect needs no dictionary, but is understood the world over." — Ralph Waldo Emerson

4. SPECIFIC FACIAL GESTURES

Very much like eye muscles, facial muscles produce gestures and expressions that can be recognized in the overall evaluation of a person's body language.[24]

A smile in and of itself means nothing, of course, since there are <u>thousands</u> of combinations of facial muscles that can form smiles of many types. It is to what the smile, and its type, reacts that give the viewer clues as to the unconscious muscular variations that speak a hidden language.[25]

Certainly, smiling at a joke or pleasant event is normal and expected. However, an inappropriate smile can be a signal of nervousness, sarcasm,

---

[24] For an excellent and comprehensive listing of almost every imaginable human gesture, and a discussion of their meanings, see Morris, Desmond, *Manwatching – A Field Guide to Human Behavior*, New York: Harry N. Abrams, Inc., 1977, at p. 24.

[25] For an extensive discussion of "facial clues to deceit," see Ekman, Paul, *Telling Lies*, previously cited, at. P. 123.

boredom, anger, or even a distractive or psychotic affect. Were a person to be asked a question of a serious nature, a responsive serious answer preceded by a very quick smile (in which a smile would definitely not be in order), becomes a signal that deception, at the least, or extreme nervousness is present, and should be pursued further.

As discussed before in looking at cultural differences, some people (especially Asian cultures) seem to Americans to use a smile as a mask when dealing with unpleasant situations. This can be a frustrating lack of knowledge for those who must deal with different cultures in difficult situations.

A smirk or frown, of course, is a sign of disdain, defiance or disapproval, and depending upon when given, should be taken as a negative gesture or one of concealment on the part of the respondent, especially if the person attempts to place one or both hands on hips. So too, blushing, constriction of facial muscles, fidgeting, or strained laughter unwittingly signal severe tension.

Finally, as to facial gestures in general, a sure-fire sign of unconscious disagreement is one's showing one's tongue in response to a question or statement. Tracing this trait back to childhood explains how sticking one's tongue out completely at another is a sign of utter mocking or disrespect. The fact is, this tongue showing, along with many other of the subliminal signs we are discussing, make their appearance in childhood, and are repressed with age as best as the person can. No one can be 100% successful at this.

5. THE MOUTH AND FACIAL CAMOUFLAGING

A person's mouth, from which truth or lies verbally flow, is another central point of body language signals that a person attempts to hide. Whether it is a subtle covering of the mouth during a statement, swallowing or gulping at an inopportune time, or an inappropriate smile or facial expression, all are used to get to the core of kinesics. These physiological signals involving the mouth, often unperceived because they occur in far less than one-half second or appear natural, are at times what can be called unconscious "micro-signals."

Throat-clearing in response to a question or statement usually signifies disagreement to something that is said or asked, to which a direct negative comment at that moment would be inappropriate. Thus, the body's making such a sound, which rarely can be consciously stifled, signifies that disagreement immediately.

Gulping at the time a response is due is a sign of nervousness, which of course should lead the questioner to probe the reason or source for that nervousness.

Smiling inappropriately at a question (again, watch out for the cultural differences I've discussed) is the body's way of unconsciously telling the truth, while the conscious mind knows a verbal non-truth is about to surface.

Something I have seen, especially as a Judge with the geographic advantage of sitting closest to the witness box and perceiving even the smallest of facial movements that might be invisible to anyone else in the room, is a question asking for an answer that could somehow implicate the responder. When a denial finally issues, I have seen at times (when it later was shown the person was lying outright at that point), the slightest burst of a smile — quickly retracted — as the serious (and untrue) answer was given.

Finally, in regard to the mouth, the most common sense defense against being perceived as lying is physically and unconsciously attempting to suppress or "cover over" the words that are actually spoken. How is this done? Simple! A *person covers his mouth with his hand as if scratching or yawning!* I cannot begin to count the times a client or witness or suspect I have seen or interviewed has found an excuse to rub his lips, scratch his mouth or nose, pull on his left ear with his right hand, run his index finger under his nostrils, scratch his nose, or in some other manner cause his hand to come between his lips and face and the questioner while an outright lie is being spoken.

Speaking of noses, the one conclusion I have repeatedly witnessed in jurors or around a conference table, is someone rubbing his nose repeatedly. Assuming from your observations that you've read this in context, (and is not merely a one-time nose itch), such a gesture almost always indicates that the person does not believe what he is hearing.

The human physiology strives always to tell the truth, regardless of the conscious intent of the person: thus, even with a verbal lie, the body's way to contradict that without the speaker's knowledge, is the traditional "mouth cover."

An excellent and very current example of how body language gives away even trained liars (also known in some circles as "diplomats"), occurred during an interview in Baghdad with Iraqi Deputy Foreign Minister Tariq Aziz, a spokeman for dictator Saddam

Hussein. Ted Koppel, on ABC's *Nightline*, inquired regarding Iraq's possession of "weapons of mass destruction," which Aziz repeatedly denied. You can see from the following three (3) photographic stills (technically called "screengrabs") from that interview taping, how the classic application of facial kinesics indicating blatant deception are present, in textbook form: repetitive mouth-covering, eyeglass adjustments, chin-scratching and face poking, all accompanied by *simultaneous breach of eye contact.*

"Copyright© ABC News – Nightline, December 4, 2002.
Reprinted with permission."

71

Marc Mogil, J.D.

In sum, when verbal and non-verbal signals diametrically clash, ALWAYS believe the non-verbal!

Finally, in the area of a unique form of natural facial camouflaging, an area of great dispute amongst kinesics practitioners over the past 30 years is the presence of a full beard. Some feel that it has become an issue of style and men's sartorial aura, while others insist that a man grows a full beard (however neatly trimmed) as a mode of camouflage or concealment of some emotional or factual indicia.

It has been my own personal experience that I must side with the latter and original, more conventional view: I have found that bearded men (with certain rare exceptions) wish some emotional or personality trait kept from the casual outsider, and is a constructive bar to ascertaining facial motions, micro-movements, and sets itself forth as a shield of a modern sort, (since we cannot get away with wearing facial armor any more).[26]

The fact that a beard is present by no means implies in and of itself that a person is less than candid. What it does mean is that there exists some substantial underlying personal trait in which the person wishes to maintain a higher than ordinary degree of privacy, and non-disclosure of potentially relevant facial movements.

Of course, we cannot include those individuals whose circumstances prevent them from being clean-shaven (religion, culture, a recent facial injury leaving a scar, poverty, etc). We are, however, speaking about those individuals who have the choice of wearing or not wearing facial hair, and take this route.

---

[26] Once again, I caution making conclusions without knowing the cultural background since, for example in some culture or religions — like the Amish in Pennsylvania, the Singh in India, Muslims, or Chasidic Jewish sects worldwide — grown men are expected to have full beards.

Questioning a bearded individual takes more of an effort and concentration, since the slight twinges and motions more easily seen on a hairless face, are much more easily concealed here.

Think of someone you know with a full beard, WHY you believe the beard was grown, and HOW the person's personality may have slightly changed after or just before it occurred. I've done this with friends and relatives whom I knew well, and have come across college professors, physicians, psychiatrists and others whose personality became a tad more secretive, less talkative and perhaps at times introverted before or as the beard grew in.

6. LIPS

Clenched, pursed or curved lips are another signal of the body trying to tell the truth.

Additionally, these clenched or pursed lips during a response, or occurring at the end of a question, usually implies extensive disagreement with the question, and at times anger. It is a sign of a tense malevolence towards the question, and more often signifies a degree of insult that the question was asked in the first place.

Raising one side of the mouth and lips after a question, or at a crucial part of the conversation, signifies disdain, disagreement, or a desire to literally mock what was just said. It is a very strong signal.

A curled bottom lip during a similar situation implies an extreme anger, and unless the reason is clear, must be pursued to ascertain the cause.[27]

---

[27] For a study of reading facial expressions and detecting insincerity, I refer you to Marsh, Peter, ed., *Eye-to-Eye — How People Interact*, Topsfield, MA: Salem House Publishers, 1988, at pp. 78 and 116.

7. HAND POSITION OR MOTION

Watching a person's hands and fingers can be almost as useful as a stare or a person's eyes, since it is impossible not to make some even slight hand motions without actually SITTING on them. (I suspect not too many people feel comfortable sitting on their hands.)

For instance, wringing of the hands or finger tapping signifies nervousness, restlessness, fear or even combativeness, and does not go so much directly to veracity, but to clues about *why* the person would be tense, nervous or angry at that particular time. What was specifically asked that produced this reaction?

Forming a so-called "finger steeple" with both hands (a triangle made with the fingers of both hands with the point facing up) manifests extreme indecision, at times superiority, or a reflective contemplation, as does stroking the chin or tilting the head while listening.

Playing continuously or repeatedly with hand jewelry, such as a ring, watch or bracelet, or tapping a pen or pencil, usually means the person is vigorously attempting to search for an answer that will satisfy his questioner, and can be a sign of extreme nervousness or deception.

A hand moved to the chest, to unconsciously cover the area of the vulnerable sternum and heart, (especially among women) is a defensive gesture, leading to follow up queries for what at that specific juncture elicited that response.

Pointing a thumb in the direction of a person clearly signifies a high degree of contempt in our society, while pointing a finger directly at someone, unless in jest, is a combative and aggressive gesture.

Placing or clasping one's hands behind the head, or on the hip when standing, most usually signifies a degree of arrogance, anger or condescension, and certainly a degree of defiance.

Finally, folding one's hands and arms in front of the body signifies respect, submissiveness, contemplation and a sense of calm. However, if you see that the grip of the hands is tight, or only occurs after certain issues are raised, it is a self-restraining action signifying extreme anger, tension, or pending deception at where the questioning is going, as well as annoyance or disbelief.

8. SPEED OF RESPONSE

The human mind is an intricate computer, analyzing each and every bit of input and unconsciously reacting as well as consciously deciding what seems best for the person at that particular moment. This is manifested verbally by the time between question and answer, and the *differences* between this "baseline time" and that of a more difficult question, or one with most severe implications.

For instance, I've asked people who were obviously very nervous, "easy" and non-stressful questions first that began with their names, where they lived, how many children they had, whether they spent recent time on vacation, what their favorite hobby was, etc. In this way, I received a sense of HOW a person responded (the "baseline" response), the tone used, the body language symbols given, and the speed of their responses to very non-threatening questions.

Thereafter, I noted on difficult questions, not only the body language symbols given, but also whether there was some *delay* in giving a response coupled with any of these signs. This is so since it has become apparent through the years that a slower than normal response, although it can certainly be someone who is thoroughly contemplating a response, often also is a means of stalling when the answer will create difficulties for them. Certainly, if you ask something that requires a detailed description, a delay is normal for the person to sort out the details. However, if what you are asking requires merely a "yes" or "no" answer, a delay manifests a distinct stalling and perhaps a deceptive and false response. Taken to an extreme, *complete* silence is a sure sign of hostility.

On the other side of the coin, a response calling for a "yes" or "no", in which the character of the speaker is somehow put into question, a very rapid, loud and clear response, with good eye contact and a body-tilt towards you, is a response of veracity virtually jumping out of the chair.

Again, I must stress that it is a combination of the symbols that are important as we get to them one-by-one, as well as a comparison to the concept of a "baseline" for each that we have discussed, that will lead to your determination.

As for the voice itself, there are of course experienced polygraphers who can – either by traditional lie detector machines, or by hidden or portable units (as set forth in "Chapter I: An

Overview)[28] ascertain the levels of stress and intonation changes during speaking. By evaluating levels of emotion, cognitive function, stress values, and thinking values, a trained vocal analyst has the technology now to assess parameters of sound made by the human voice, monitor changes in stress indications to specific questions, and quickly make conclusions regarding avoidance, uncertainty, excitement or false statements.

However, that subject is a book in and of itself.

---

[28] There now exist subminiature hand-held machines, also attachable to cell phones, weighing no more than 45 grams and no longer than 83 centimeters, available to the public as I write this, that can make these rough calculations after proper calibration, (see, for example, the portable lie detector *Handy Truster* ™ TNF-100, manufactured by 911 Computer Co, Ltd., in Seoul, South Korea, for US distribution).

9. CHIN AND JAW POSITION

The chin and jaw play a role in body language interpretation, as do any other muscle movements in the facial mask. For instance, a jutting chin signifies anger or aggression; a chin that is raised so that they eyes seem to look at a downward angle implies an attitude of superiority, annoyance, arrogance or even disdain; a chin tucked into the chest is a defensive contraction, and certainly not a positive gesture.

When in a clenched, biting position, the mouth tells the observer that the person is reacting in a very angry, controlled manner. And as we've already discussed, stroking of the chin is an evaluative and neutral posture.

10. THE ARMS

The arms and hands, moving in conjunction with other non-verbal actions of the body, are an encyclopedia of kinesics. The main ones have repeated themselves so very often in my years that they've become almost second nature, including those we've already covered.

Consider someone sitting with arms in his lap: when asked a question, the arms are suddenly crossed and locked tightly. This signifies a defensive and antagonistic position, one of disagreement and of "I want to block out what you're saying."

When arms are held at one's side or on one's lap, it symbolizes an openness and willingness to observe and consider. When the arms and hands are placed on or towards the hips or clutched behind the head, one can be assured that there exists a degree of anger and defiance that must be explored.

Finally, as one can surmise if dealing with a person in any capacity over a period of time, the sudden clench of the hands into fists signify that under any less civilized setting, a violent response would be contemplated, while rubbing them together manifests an extreme disbelief.

11. THE LEGS

Watching someone's legs give many clues to the way a person feels. Crossing them in the direction of another person indicates openness towards them, while crossing them away from the person just the opposite.

Rocking the legs or tapping the feet repetitively indicates an extraordinary nervousness, which, if coupled with a specific question, means that the subject is in some way reluctant to respond and is upset with the possibilities.

Most importantly, legs that are crossed while the arms are *also* crossed (with perhaps the slightest hint of a frown), makes clear this person is combative, in disagreement, or rejects *in toto* whatever is being then said.

12. HEAD MOTIONS

The final area of consideration in our analysis is the motion of the head, however so slight it may be.

Of course, every child here in America learns with age that a symbol for "yes" or "I agree" is an up-and-down motion of the head, while a "no" or "I disagree" is a motion from side-to-side.[29] Using this childhood motion in an adult can be quite startling, since studies have shown that someone asked questions ALWAYS physiologically moves their head for several tenths of a second to indicate comprehension by the brain of the query ("synchrony.") [30] The brain causes the head, and the rest of the body, to unconsciously also mimic the

---

[29] Remember, again, that in some cultures, this sign is REVERSED, and a "yes" or affirmative motion can be movement of the head from side-to-side instead.

[30] Traditionally defined as occurring when the speaker and listener are in agreement, and the speaker's rhythmic movements are mimicked; "simultaneous occurrences" or "the concurrence of events in time," *The American Heritage ®Dictionary of the English Language*, 4th ed., New York: Houghton Mifflin Company, 2000.

motions of someone they agree with. They'll swear that no such motion took place, but showing such a person a videotape often causes extreme surprise at what motions were indeed made.

For instance, if after a series of questions, the responding party sees the speaker, with whom he agrees or respects, scratch his arm, watch carefully and you can see the person ultimately mimicking the action. If you ask later if he did so, he will honestly emphatically deny it.

However, head motion — depending on direction — manifests an unconscious signal of agreement or disagreement.

Quite clearly, someone who answers "yes" while initially slightly shaking their head from side-to-side is really saying "no," and visa versa.

If any general rule can be taken from this book as **"The Mogil Rule,"** it is:

If it is a choice between the words and the body language, the body language always tells the truth.

However, a general principle to remember in studying body language is that the human mind has been conditioned for thousands of years to react in some way with a head motion after every statement or question is posed — synchrony. *If one realizes this alone in studying people, you have gone behind their protective masks guarding inner thought.*

Aside from what has been discussed previously, nodding the head after each such prompt is a signal of both attentiveness and understanding, usually reflecting receptiveness. Any other head movement should provoke immediate attention.

Looking away after a direct question calling for a direct answer, or while addressing someone else, is a signal of at least a partial deception or feeling "exposed." This is so since the movement of the head away from the other person includes aversion of direct eye contact also, and they usually are congruent to each other in an analysis of someone's body language.

* * * *

Chapter III

Non-Verbal Signals: Territoriality and Zones of Privacy

In any study of body language by a layperson, there are issues of "proxemics" (the science of spatial relationships, "territoriality" and "zones of privacy" created by human beings in order to feel comfortable in various situations, as defined previously (and used by Professor Hall in 1963) that must serve as a mandatory preface to the first of the symbols we'll look into, that of body position.

Every human being worldwide creates in his mind a private geographic area (the zone of privacy) surrounding oneself, in any business, social or family situation, which — if intruded upon — creates discomfort and primeval and unconscious fear. As a species, we are highly territorial and are consciously and unconsciously cognizant of spatial relationships between people. They can be "formal" or fixed (like walls or a desk), or "informal," a so-called human initiated invisible "bubble" surrounding a person.

In the United States, a typical area that a person requires to be comfortable in his own little space is approximately 3-5 feet surrounding him in all directions, (while, for example, I've found those raised in Middle Eastern, South or Central American cultures set far less of a distance to be comfortable). If broached, one can immediately sense the negative and nervous reaction to the intrusion.[31]

If we look at *any* two people standing in conversation in the street, we can see that the distance

---

[31] See a very interesting study online by author John Mole, entitled *"Decoding Body Language,"* for further insight, ("http://www.johnmole.com/articles18b.htm").

between them remains relatively constant. As one may move inwards or away, the other seems to mirror the motion in order to keep the distance fairly constant, almost like a dance.

Likewise, when people move into an elevator, subway car, bus or room, watch to see how they separate themselves almost like random molecules to all areas of the space, and place articles of clothing or personal items on nearby bordering seats, if available, thereby giving themselves a block of space. This is very similar in physics to the concept of "molecular diffusion," in which molecules or other atomic particles fill up in an even pattern of dispersal of a gas randomly, (related to the "Kinetic theory of gases.").[32]

---

[32] To the scientifically minded, might I suggest an excellent text on this topic, Beiser, Arthur, *Physics,* 5th ed., Reading, MA: Addision-Wesley Publishing Company, 1991, at pp. 357-366.

This "territoriality" of a human being is defined formally in science as the "zone of privacy" which one unconsciously must maintain in order to continue to feel comfortable. It is a subliminal nuance as old as our species, when our ancestors staked out their own caves. Tribal societies always have set borders upon what they deemed to be their territories, and history is replete with examples of angry exchanges resulting from perceived violation of this space.

A perfect example of how this is used to gain the upper hand in non-verbal communication is during a skilled police or CIA interrogation of a suspect. Normally, standard purely informational interviews are done seated at a table or desk of some sort between the parties, and can occur in the person's home or office. This makes both people comfortable, since it creates the buffer required to maintain a degree of bodily privacy.

However, if the Agent wishes to try to strip away defenses to the discussion, there will only be CHAIRS in the interrogation room, so that the questioning officer can sit closer (or even stand above the subject) than the person's border of his zone of privacy, unconsciously piercing it, and face him or her directly, glaring at him throughout. His voice pitch will be higher than normal, indicating a hostile disbelief. By dong so, not only is intentional stress and discomfort created, but the officer assumes a dominant position and may ultimately elicit information that might not ordinarily have been proffered.

Additionally, by having the questioning in a previously unseen governmental facility, rather than the person's home, the additional comfort factor of geographic familiarity is removed. *Ergo*, more stress to the target.

A great deal of the time, experienced interviewers or trial lawyers begin with simple and easy-to-answer questions asked (with a smile, pleasant visage and very soft voice) from about 15-20 feet away, with the questioner skilled in proxemics and territoriality moving ever closer with each more difficult question, very slightly raising the pitch of his voice with each. This proceeds until the potential answers become highly controversial and central to the issue at hand, at which time the questioner has penetrated well within the target's zone of privacy, has totally and intentionally breached his territoriality, and is speaking in a much louder than normal tone of voice. All this together often "softens" the "on-guard" resistance of a suspect or a hostile witness into a more cooperative or implicative mode, in which the body language signals become far more pronounced and exaggerated, easier to "read," and at times leading to verbal errors by the responding party.

Finally, another tactic utilized by skilled interrogators or attorneys during trial, is the practice of *absolute silence* at an awkward moment. Psychiatrists frequently do the same, for the same result: it tends to provoke a nervous or anxious response, and a sustained silence may evince an implicative word, phrase or statement that would not otherwise have been given.

Chapter IV

The Ideal Candidates for Practicing Non-Verbal Communication

With all we now know concerning the beginnings of the study of human body language, it is important to realize that what we use most frequently in receiving cues about other people (aside from our brains, of course): these are our *eyes*. Without seeing and observing the sometimes-minute bodily movements of subjects, we would be helpless in this art. It is the most necessary sense utilized in the study of kinesics or proxemics.

Well, what about our other senses: hearing, smell, touch, and taste? Most are useless in reading non-verbal communication, except for hearing, since the mind by sound can detect deviations in tones, air-intake, and therefore lies.

Of course, one could argue that a tense person perspires more and one can sense that by the sense of smell, or that someone's slight quiver or muscle twitch, which sends a signal could be felt with the sense of touch. However, assigning that even a number as high as 1% is being rather generous with those talents. It is largely SEEING that makes a successful body language expert.

Well, if that is the case, do we need the other senses at all (except to a smaller degree hearing) to practice this craft? It is this writer's experience that the answer is an emphatic "no." Thus, the logical conclusion that follows is that someone who has been somehow forced to develop the sense of sight to the exclusion of any

Marc Mogil, J.D.

other, would be better at it than someone who possesses all of their senses. Why is this so?

Human physiology has evolved to the state that when a person is either born without or loses one of these senses, there is an automatic *compensation* in the human body, making the other senses far more acute, with "intact modalities improv[ing] in order to counteract the lost input."[33] Thus, if one cannot see, the sense of hearing becomes, for example, far superior to the average person's.

The conclusion from this premise is that in the study of kinesics, a person without the sense of hearing whatsoever makes potentially a more adept practitioner of reading body language with the eyes. This has been observed since a physiologic absence of

---

[33] See, for example, a colloquium abstract of a paper presented before the Planck Institute in Tubingen, Germany, by Roeder, Brigitte (Ph.D.), of the Philipps Universitaet, Marburg, Germany, entitled, *Spatial Behavior Without Vision*, November 22, 2002, [translated into English].

hearing forces the person to concentrate on the main sensory input remaining — sight and observation. And it is through sight that the signs, cues, gestures and symbols of body language mainly manifest themselves. A deaf person is not "handicapped" in his study of body language by a (to others) distractive sense of hearing. The person instead hones in on every detailed movement of the person being studied. In actual day-to-day living, the developed sense of sight and compensatory technology on everyday appliances assist the deaf person to successfully navigate a world in which noises normally are quite important to survival (hearing honking of horns, ringing of phones and doorbells, conversation, etc).

It is therefore no surprise that one will find that those people who can almost on cue *block out* hearing when studying someone's body language, can often be the most thorough and accomplished at it.

It is for this reason, in my work now as the President of a jury selection consulting firm, I sometimes suggest to trial attorneys to retain a deaf individual (usually someone with training and experience in clinical psychology) to sit in the courtroom with us, and provide input as to what they "hear" from the jury and witnesses with their more observant eyes. They then write out what they conclude after each session.

Chapter V

Test Yourself!

Now that we've touched upon the major areas of body language, an excellent and time-tested way of solidifying your understanding and application of the principles set forth, are to *test* them personally in a non-embarrassing setting, (I won't ask you to sit and stare at strangers on a subway!)

What you should do, if you're a young associate in a law firm, or someone who is merely interested in acquiring this useful skill, is the following: go to your local video store, and rent a movie which you've been meaning to see but haven't. (Avoid "shoot-em-ups," Kung Fu movies, animation, slapstick comedies, etc...stick to plots with full story lines or romantic films). YOU WILL BE WATCHING THIS MOVIE WITH A FEW COLLEAGUES OR A FRIEND OR SPOUSE. You'll also being watching this movie twice. The first viewing (a lot of work), without any sound whatsoever: the second time normally with sound. Take either the DVD or videotape, along with a pad and pen, and find comfortable chairs. Minimize distractions in the room. What you're about to do is see how thoroughly the symbols discussed are enmeshed in any movie involving the motion and speaking of human beings, and how well you can apply them to understand what is being said without hearing a word of dialog. TURN OFF THE SOUND.

At the top of your pad, make five (5) columns, entitled "SCENE," "CHARACTER" "TYPE OF NON-VERBAL COMMUNICATION," "PLOT INDICATION," and "PERSONALITY TRAIT."

Under "SCENE," write as the movie progresses a brief line about where or what is taking place. You'll do that with each scene in the film.

Next to it, list what characters appear. The third column is where you will note any types of body language you read from what you are watching (i.e. – anger, stares, pursed lips, apparent shouting, crossed arms, interchanges using the cues or gestures that we've discussed, and anything else you can think of). For simplicity's sake (so that you can keep your concentration on the film), this should be by your own notational symbols for specific acts, such as:

⬭⬭ = eyes (stare, looking away, covered by hand, etc., modified to adapt each;

⬭⬭ = eyebrows

✗ = leg or leg cross

= hands or fists

 = shoulders (angularity)

 = mouth

 = entire body, or done tilted as indicated

 = responsive head movement

 = arms open or crossed

I'll allow you to use your own imagination and artistic talents to create your own codified symbols for all the rest that you may wish to record, or you may wish to refer to established scientists expert in the

field who have devised complex sets of these
symbols.[34]

The initial time this is done, it may seem very
difficult, with constant writing and attempting to
correlate the action to your notes. Do your best, but
don't be concerned, since when you finish the first
viewing, you'll then analyze what you've written, make
conclusions as to what exactly you think the movie was
about in detail, what the characters' personalities were
like, and what the entire film was trying to put forth.

Compare your notes with your friend, spouse or
colleague, and see where you differed and WHY. After
you discuss the differences and possible reasons, note
those also in detail.

Give yourselves reasonable time (not too long) for a
break, whip up some microwave popcorn, sit *without*

---

[34] See, for excellent suggestions, the leading expert in this particular

any pen or pencil, and watch the entire movie normally.

I GUARANTEE YOU WILL BE VERY PLEASANTLY SURPRISED AT HOW MUCH YOU "READ" FROM THE SILENT VERSION. Of course, on a first attempt, it will not be as complete, totally correct, nor as detailed as an expert's, but as compared to someone who has *never* delved into the signs, symbols and gestures of body language, it will be an amazing perception of what transpired, and you will be correct far more often than not. *Try it!*

The first time is always the most impactive upon your mind. From there, it only gets better and better, and you will find yourself attempting the same thing, in your mind, when you deal with people in your everyday life.

---

field, Birdwhistell's, *Kinesic and Context,* as cited previously.

Chapter VI

Conclusion

I don't know about you, but when my family and I go on vacation, I like to totally unwind, relax and change the routines I follow normally. I make certain I never see a newspaper, watch local TV, or take files with me to work on during a hiatus in some nice, warm spot. The only decisions I wish to make involve where my family and I, for instance, will be dining that night, or what beach or other island or attraction should be visited on a particular day. I certainly don't want any part of law or body language analysis interfering with my private time.

However, wiping the on-guard work slate from my mind is very difficult for two reasons: first,

I was brought up as a streetwise New York City kid, who never let his guard down and always was aware of his surroundings; second, my interest and training in body language cannot be turned off like a faucet. The mind just doesn't quit on demand.

To illustrate my first point, let me share an embarrassing incident of my past: on arrival in Bloomington, Indiana, to attend Indiana University Law School in 1970, I met a few interesting people in classes and the graduate dormitory, and we decided that first Sunday to catch breakfast in "downtown" Bloomington, instead of the dormitory cafeteria.

First, you have to understand that this wonderful "Big Ten" town, then comprised of 30,000 students and 30,000 local resident citizens, was a typical Midwestern locale, with a central town square village green, containing a City Hall and all other governmental offices, surrounded by old war memorials and statues and traditional little shops of all sorts that had been there for years.

As we walked on the square (5 of us from Indiana, Illinois, Iowa and Missouri, and me from New York), I spotted two men and a woman, in their late 30's or early 40's, walking towards us: with my New York City sixth sense, I noticed they were changing their path so that our two groups would intersect momentarily. Sensing a threat of some sort, (perhaps a mugging?), I immediately started to change paths and move slightly away from our course, and put my hand over my back pocket containing my wallet and ID. Yet, still they came towards us nonetheless! As we were almost upon each other, they stopped in front of us, smiled, and said "Morning! — Isn't it a lovely Sunday?" (And they *meant* it, these warm "townies").

The point: I was thoroughly embarrassed and ashamed at my fearful and anticipatory attitude, since my survivalist New York City street instincts placed a perceived threat in front of us that certainly did not exist. Awful! It took me years to live that down, (especially to myself).

As to a second example, I recall one winter many years later on a St. Martin (Maarten) beach. We were sitting comfortably on a white sandy area behind our hotel, and I was comfortably ensconced in an almost horizontal lounge chair, with large straw hats, sunglasses and the compulsory rum swizzles. The beach was relatively secluded with about 30 or so hotel guests, and I was trying my darndest to think only about the incoming waves, the puffy white clouds and — in the 85-degree weather — the snow, slush and cold winds we had left behind at LaGuardia Airport in New York City.

However, something was unconsciously tugging at my concentration, and it distracted me. Finally, what it was dawned: I was unwittingly interpreting a conversation between a man and his apparent wife some 150 feet away, and it wasn't at all a pleasant discussion. Yet, I could clearly tell the general nature of the conversation, which was the more assertive of the two, and what the likely outcome would be (without hearing a word).

As I tried to "turn it off," I began to realize for the first time that once one acquires such a "language," like any other language or skill, it *cannot be turned off at will*. Like an infernal machine whose "off" switch wouldn't work, I was "on" all the time. This continued at the pool later with another group of strangers, at dinner when we sat a few tables away from people who, to me at least, spoke primarily with their hands, and at a casino where I could have been wearing earmuffs and it wouldn't have made a bit of difference. (I think I made the pit boss at the blackjack tables a bit uneasy).

I ultimately realized after that vacation that one skilled at body language, as any other talent, cannot completely turn it off, nor should they, since it becomes a second-nature protective ability. If I had wanted to minimize its effects. I would have had to put most people physically behind me on the beach, or take a chair in the dining room facing my family alone and a wall, and not outward towards the rest of the room.

Although this would have worked then, and although in succeeding years I still can't "turn off" at will, I *do* know how to consciously place myself in a position where my eyes and reading of body language cannot work as well as if I absolutely do not wish that skill to be available to me.

I hope most of you interested in this field as I was as a college student, find a hobby to engage in that will allow you, too, to take your mind away from body language analysis if you wish it when your skill dramatically increases and you feel the need for some respite. And, of course, I *primarily* wish you great success and enjoyment in attaining this developing skill in the first place!

In the meantime, as a conclusion to this particular work, might I suggest that your best practice, other than the task I suggested as an example of movie interpretation, is to tie the words of people you thoroughly know (close relatives or friends) to their actions, so you can see the non-verbal correlations more clearly and test the body language assumptions we've discussed.

Also, in office politics situations, watch your supervisors at meetings to detect body language gestures, look around conference tables, and make it a point to try to project whatever image you think appropriate in various situations.

Young attorneys or those seeking a career in jury consulting should make it a point to watch experienced trial attorneys select juries in serious cases: this is excellent for both the experience, and the fact that there is no pressure whatsoever on the observer. (No senior partner or client is around to evaluate your work!) Scroll from jury to witness, to defendant, to prosecutor, to defense lawyer, to judge. Take what may seem to you as senseless notes and memos to yourself regarding motions, positions, angularity, eye contact, leg crossing, and all the other gestures discussed, which you will coordinate later. Watch them all carefully, and try to find signs of kinesics and proxemics with which we've dealt: you'll find many if not all of them even during your first viewing of a complete trial.

Your *other* important task, should you seek this out as a career, is a MORAL one: in my lifetime, I have made it a point to understand that there will always be those experts available who will, for the right price, TV coverage and other publicity, aid *anyone* in the jury selection process, no matter how overwhelming and heinous the offense alleged, or the unique repugnance of a particular defendant coupled with overwhelming physical evidence of his guilt and underlying motive and opportunity. In recent years, I personally have made a conscious decision that I cannot in good faith (to the client *or* myself) apply my abilities and experience in cases involving, for instance, the overt onerous relatively recent tactic of playing of a "race card" as a central theme to a celebrity homicide defense, or of a caught-in-the-act serial child mass murderer, no matter how large the remuneration (some times in the high six figures or low seven figures!)

Perhaps this type of rationale is a moral breach or flaw in my own personality, and self-inflicted financial idiocy...perhaps not. Each person in the process must not only become adept at the substantive craft, but must also come to terms with severe and everlasting issues of conscience and the ability to look at oneself in the mirror after each case.

I Know What You're Really Thinking
Be grateful that you're not the defendant, and learn

from the process.

REFERENCES

Beiser, Arthur, Physics, 5th ed., Reading, MA: Addison-Wesley Publishing Company, 1991.

Birdwhistell, Ray I., *Kinesics and Context,* Philadelphia: University of Pennsylvania Press, 1970;

Darwin, Charles, *The Expression of Emotions in Man and Animals,* New York: St. Martin's Press, 1980;

Dimitrius, Jo-Ellan and Mazzarella, Mark Reading People: How to Understand People and Predict Their Behavior Anytime, Anyplace, New York: Ballantine Books, 1999

Ekman, Paul & Friesen, Wallace, *Unmasking the Face,* Englewood Cliffs, NJ: Prentice-Hall, Inc., 1975;

Ekman, Paul, *Telling Lies: Clues to Deceit in the Marketplace, Politics and Marriage,* New York: W.W. Norton & Co., 2001;

Fast, Julius, *Body Language,* New York: Evans & Co., 1970;

Franken, Stephanie, *Body Language Often Tells Another Story,* The Topeka-Capital Journal Newspaper, April 30, 2001;

Givens, Robert B., *The Nonverbal Dictionary of Gestures, Signs & Body Language Cues (from Adam's-Apple-Jump to Zygomatic Smile),*

Marc Mogil, J.D.

Spokane, Washington: Center for Nonverbal Studies Press, 2002;

Krauss, Elissa and Bonora, Beth (eds), <u>Jurywork: Systematic Techniques Volumes 1 and</u> 2nd ed., New York: National Jury Project, 1992.

Kressel, Neil J. and Kressel Dorit F., <u>Stack and Sway: The New Science of Jury Consulting</u>, Boulder: Westview Press, 2002.

Hinde, Robert A., *Non-Verbal Communication,* London: Cambridge University Press, 1972;

Luscher, Max, *Color Test,* New York: Pocket Books, Inc, 1971;

Marsh, Peter, ed., *Eye-to-Eye: How People Interract,* Topsfield, MA: Salem House Publishers, 1988;

Mehrabian, Albert, *Nonverbal Communication,* Chicago: Aldine –Atherton, Inc., 1972;

Mole, John, *Decoding Body Language,* online on the World Wide Web at johnmole.com/articles18b.htm;

Morris Desmond, *Bodytalk: The Meaning of Human Gestures,* New York: Crown Trade Paperbacks, 1995;

Morris Desmond, *Gestures: Their Origins and Distribution,* New York: Stein & Day, 1980;

Morris, Desmond, *Body Talk,* New York: Crown Trade Paperbacks, 1994;

Morris, Desmond, *Manwatching – A Field Guide to Human Behavior,* New York: Harry N. Abrams, Inc., 1977;

Nierenberg, Gerald I. & Colero, Henry H., *How to Read a Person Like a Book,* New York: Friedman, Michael Publishing Group, 2002;

Roeder, Brigitte, *Spatial Behavior Without Vision,* abstract of a paper presented at the Planck Institute in Tubingen Germany, November 22, 2002.

Spiegel, Joseph P. & Machotka, Pavel, *Messages of the Body,* New York: The Free Press, 1974;

The American Heritage® Dictionary of the English Language 4th ed., New York: Houghton Mifflin Co, 2000;

USAF Museum, Presidential Aircraft Museum, http://www.upafb.af.mil/museum/annex/an32.htm/2002

Vrij, Aldert, Detecting Lies and Deceit: The Psychology of Lying and the Implication for Professional Practice, Chichester: John Wiley & Sons (Europe), 2000;

Marc Mogil, J.D.

INDEX
========================

=====

ABC-TV
Affect, 42, 63
Aggressive, 36, 37, 80
Air Force One, 15
Anger, 18, 33, 53, 63, 76, 77, 80, 85, 87, 107
Angularity, 33, 34, 108, 119
Antennae, 32
Architects, 29
Argumentative, 46
Armani®, 44
Arms, 9, 10, 13, 17, 18, 80, 86, 88, 108
Arrogance, 80, 85
Asians, 63
Assertiveness, 13
Attire, 10, 26, 41, 44
Audible, 21
Audio tape, 21
Authority, 27, 29, 40, 44, 45, 46
Aziz, Tariq, 68
Baseball, 16, 18
Baseline, 4, 7, 9, 81, 82, 83
Beard(s), 73, 74, 75
Beiser, Arthur, 121
Berrigan, Father, xiv
Betrayal of feeling, 54
Bible, 29
Big Ten, 112
Birdwhistell, Ray L., xiv, 121
Black, 23, 41, 43
Blinking eye, 55

Bloomington, Indiana, 112, 130
Blushing, 64
Body Language, xii, xiv, xv, 2, 5, 7, 8, 14, 15, 16, 18, 19, 26, 31, 36, 39, 44, 48, 50, 52, 53, 56, 62, 65, 82, 85, 91, 92, 93, 99, 100, 101, 103, 104, 105, 107, 110, 111, 112, 116, 117, 118, 130
Body position, 35, 37, 93
Bodytalk, 5, 122
Bonora, Beth, 121
Brain, 89
Bubbles, 94
Business meeting example, 7, 9
Camouflaging, 73
Candid, 74
Carrying, 26, 28, 29, 30, 44
CCNY, xiii
Ceiling, 23
Central Intelligence Agency, 1
Chair(s), 2, 3, 10, 11, 12, 15, 23, 35, 36, 54, 60, 83, 114, 116
Check off, 60
Chest, 79, 85
Chicago Seven, The, xiv
Chin, 79, 85
Chin-Scratching
CIA, 1, 2, 21, 96
City College of New York, xiii
Clasped, 80

Clothing, 26, 40, 44, 46, 95
Club, 41
Cognitive, 14, 84
Colero, Henry H., 50, 122
College, 41, 75, 117
Colors, 39, 40
Common sense, 14, 67
Communication, xi, 7
Compendium, xv
Compensation, 102
Condescension, 80
Conscious, 1, 19, 24, 43, 52,
  66, 68, 120
Consultant, xi, 27
Contemplation, 79, 80
Contemplative, 79, 80
Context, 9, 31, 41, 46, 68
Context-oriented, 31
Context-sensitive, 31
Control, 12, 13, 21, 24, 50, 61
Cooperative, 99
Covering mouth, 65
Covers face, 23
Crossed arms, 107
Crossed legs, 107, 119
Cues, 14, 19, 100, 103, 107
Cultural, xii, 8, 10, 22, 31, 41,
  63, 66, 74
Dance club, 41
Darwin, Charles, xiii, 121
Davis, Angela, xiv
Deaf, deafness, 103, 104
Deception, 14, 53, 63, 79, 80,
  92
Defensive, 3, 12, 55, 79, 85, 86
Defiance, 63, 80, 87
Desires, 20
Desk, 2, 15, 94, 96
Dictionary, xv, 61

Dimitrius, Jo-Ellan, 121
Disapproval, 63
Disdain, 33, 43, 63, 76, 85
Disrespect, 18, 64
Dominance, 12, 13, 36
Dominant, 12, 97
Dressed, 26, 41, 57
Ear rings, 44, 45
Eastwood, Clint, 53
Education, 27
Ekman, Paul, 5, 26, 62, 121
Emotion, 9, 49, 56, 84
Engineer, 28
Equivocal response, 25
Evasiveness, 33, 36, 54
Expression(s), 62, 65
External stimuli, 14
Eye contact, 14, 15, 36, 59, 83,
  92, 119
Eye-contact, breached
Eye motion, 52
Eye(s), 6, 10, 11, 12, 14, 15,
  23, 29, 30, 34, 36, 49, 50,
  51, 52, 53, 54, 55, 58, 59,
  61, 62, 78, 83, 85, 92, 100,
  102, 104, 107, 117, 119
Face-Poking
Facial expressions, xi, xii, 77
Facial mask, 85
Facial muscles, 62, 64
Fast, Julius, xiii, 121
FBI, 21
Feelings, 5, 8, 20, 22, 24, 26,
  36, 49
Fiction, 29
Fidgeting, 64
Finger, 10, 13, 67, 78, 80
Finger steeple, 78
Fist, 16

Flit, 55
Focus groups, 19
Folding, 80
Franken, Stephanie, 60, 121
Freud, Sigmund, 1
Friesen, Wallace, 26, 121
Frown, 63, 88
Gaze, 52, 53, 58
Gestures, xi, xiii, xv, 2, 7, 9,
    13, 14, 17, 40, 61, 62, 64,
    103, 107, 110, 118, 119
Givens, Robert B., xv, 121
Graphologist, 21
Gravity, 36
Grid, 3
Groomed, 26
Guiliani, Rudy, 58
Gulping, 65
Hall, E.T., xii
Hands, 9, 11, 23, 37, 54, 64,
    78, 80, 86, 87, 108, 116
Head, 3, 10, 22, 34, 43, 60, 79,
    80, 86, 89, 90, 91, 92, 108
Head shaking, 90, 91
Hinde, Robert A., 20, 122
Hip(s), 64, 80, 86
Hostility, 36, 83
Human organism, 19
Inappropriate smile, 62, 65
Indecision, 79
Indiana University Law
    School, 112
Indignation, 36
Inferiority, 42
Instincts, 114
Intelligence, 21
Interact, 13, 14
Interrogation, 4, 14, 60, 96, 97
Intonation, 25, 84

Jacket, 10, 11, 12, 57
Jaw, 85
Jewelry, 42, 79
Johnson, Lyndon B., 15
Journal, 28
Judgments, 43
Jury consultant, xii
Kinesics, xi, 8, 9, 52, 65, 73,
    86, 100, 102, 119
Knees, 6
Koppel, Ted, 69
Kressel, Dorit F., 122
Kressel, Neil J., 122
Kung Fu, 105
Language, xii, 9, 18, 19, 26,
    48, 62, 91, 103, 115
Lanley, VA, 1
Lapel pin, 27, 42, 44
Law firm, 105, 131
Leading, xiv, 50, 79, 99, 109
Leakage, 24
Lean, 35, 54
Legs, 88
Lie, 3, 49, 55, 67, 68, 83, 84
Lie Detector, 49, 83, 84
Lips, 11, 13, 67, 76, 107
Loyalty, 44
Lusher, Max, xiii, 122
Machotka, Pavel, 52, 123
Malevolence, 76
Marsh, Peter, 77, 122
Mask, 63
Mason, Perry, 23
Mathematicians, 29
Mayor, 58
Mazzarella Mark, 121
Mehrabian, Albert, 54, 122
Membership pin, 27
Messages, xii, 21, 42

Michigan, 41

Micro-rapid reactions, 14

Mimic, 89

Mind, 9, 11, 13, 14, 24, 26, 42, 49, 50, 51, 66, 81, 91, 93, 101, 110, 111, 112, 117

Mocking, 64

Mogil Rule, The, 91

Mole, John, 122

Molecular diffusion, 95

Moral, 27, 120

Morris, Desmond, 122

Mouth, 65, 67, 68, 76, 85, 108

Movements, xi, 2, 53, 66, 73, 74, 85, 100

Movie, 105, 107, 109, 110, 117

Muscles, 14, 49, 50, 55, 61, 62

Negative, 3, 25, 36, 63, 65, 94

Nervous, 14, 78, 81, 94, 99

Nervous system, 14

Nierenberg, Gerald I., 50, 122

Nightline

Nixon, Richard M.

Non-verbal communication, iii, xii, 5, 7, 8, 14, 31, 96, 100, 130

Non-verbal language, 18

Nose, 67, 68

Nose-Rubbing

Nostrils, 67

Novel(s), 29

Pastels, 39

Perry Mason®, 23

Personality, 48, 73, 75, 120

Physics, 95

Physiological(al, ally), 3, 14, 19, 50, 65, 89

Piercings, 45

Pitch, 98

Pittsburgh Post-Gazette, 60

Planck Institute, 102, 122

Pliable, 28

Police, 22, 45, 96

Polygraph(ers), 2, 49, 83

Postures, xii

Power, 12

Primeval, 93

Privacy, 74, 93, 96, 97, 98

Proclivities, 47

Proxemics, xii, 93, 98, 100, 119

Psychotic, 63

Race Card, 120

Reading body language, 9, 61, 102

Reading material, 27, 45, 47, 58

Receptiveness, 27, 92

Red, 17, 30, 39, 40

Rejection, 36

Religious symbols, 27

Resignation, 13

Response, 19, 33, 49, 50, 52, 53, 54, 55, 56, 64, 65, 66, 76, 79, 82, 83, 87, 99

Rhythmic movements, 89

Ring, 11, 79

Roeder, Brigitte, 102, 122

Romance novel, 28

Rub, 67

Schulman, Jay, xiii

Science fiction novel, 28

Scientific, xv, 28

Scientist, 28

Scratch, 67, 90

Scratching, 67

Senses, 100, 101, 102

Serial Child Murderers, 120
Shaking, 22, 90
Shoulders, 6, 33, 34, 54, 108
Silence, 83, 99
Sixth sense, 113
Slump, 11
Smiles, 6, 62
Smirk, 63
Socks, 39, 40
Son, iii, 41
Sound, 65, 84, 101, 106
Spatial relationships, xii, 93, 94
Spiegel, John, 52, 123
Spiritualism, 29
Starbucks example, 6, 8
Stare, 11, 13, 54, 56, 78, 105, 107
Staring, 53, 54, 56, 58
State of mind, 27
Statisticians, 29
Status, 9, 43, 44, 48
Stress, 83, 84, 97, 98
Stroking, 79, 85
Subliminal, 13, 64, 96
Submittal, 13
Sunglasses, 50, 114
Superiority, 36, 41, 79, 85
Suppress, 53, 67
Swallowing, 65
Symbols, 14, 19, 25, 31, 61, 82, 83, 93, 103, 106, 107, 108, 110
Synchrony, 89, 91
Tapping, 78, 79, 88
Tattoos, 45, 46
Territoriality, xii, 93, 96, 98
The Mogil Rule, 91
The New Republic®, 45

The Village Voice®, 45
The Wall Street Journal®, 44
Threat, 57, 113, 114
Throne, 15, 36
Thumb, 16, 22, 79
Thumbs-up, 22
Tone, 54, 82, 98
Tongue, 64
Topeka Capital-Journal, 121
Torso, 3, 33, 35
Trial consultant, xi, xii, xiv, 24, 30, 39, 42, 45, 98, 99, 104, 118, 130, 131
Truthfulness, 35, 53
Unconscious, xii, 1, 12, 14, 25, 31, 37, 40, 43, 52, 53, 62, 64, 65, 90, 93
University of Rochester, 57
Veracity, 24, 33, 52, 53, 78, 83
Verbiage, 25
Video, 105
Vocal Analyst, 84
Vocal tone signature, 2
Voice pitch, 97
Voir dire, xi, 25
Vrij, Aldert, 5, 123
Watches, jewelry, 42, 79
Wedding bands, 44
Wringing hands, 78
Zones of privacy, xii, 93

About The Author

Born and raised in New York City and educated in both New York and Bloomington, Indiana, Marc Mogil practiced trial law for a total of 25 years in New York and Florida. He was elected a New York State Judge at the age of 36, presiding over numerous homicides, robberies, and other major felonies for almost 10 of those 25 years.

A speaker on body language and the psychology of jury selection, he was previously a Special Assistant Attorney General -Office of Special Prosecutor for Medicaid Fraud Control in New York. He has written for professional legal journals and lectured to lawyers and students on the art of non-verbal communication.

No longer practicing law, he currently serves as President of JURY SELECTION CONSULTANTS, a company providing jury selection consulting in support of trial law firms in high-profile cases nationwide.

An instrument rated airplane pilot and pianist in his spare time, he resides with his wife and large family in Great Neck, New York.